CINEGEEK

FUN TRIVIA TIDBITS CELEBRATING THE CINEMATIC WORLD

Become our fan on Facebook **facebook.com/idwpublishing**
Follow us on Twitter **@idwpublishing**
Subscribe to us on YouTube **youtube.com/idwpublishing**
See what's new on Tumblr **tumblr.idwpublishing.com**
Check us out on Instagram **instagram.com/idwpublishing**

WRITTEN AND ILLUSTRATED BY
PLUTTARK

TRANSLATED BY
BRANDON KANDER

EDITED BY
JUSTIN EISINGER

PRODUCTION BY
CRYSSY CHEUNG

PUBLISHER
TED ADAMS

ISBN: 978-1-63140-900-4   20 19 18 17   1 2 3 4

Ted Adams, CEO & Publisher
Greg Goldstein, President & COO
Robbie Robbins, EVP/Sr. Graphic Artist
Chris Ryall, Chief Creative Officer
David Hedgecock, Editor-in-Chief
Matthew Ruzicka, CPA, Chief Financial Officer
Lorelei Bunjes, VP of Digital Services
Jerry Bennington, VP of New Product Development

PLUTTARK

CINEGEEK

FUN TRIVIA TIDBITS CELEBRATING THE CINEMATIC WORLD

If you sit through all the credits
for a hidden scene; or if you like
stories about vampire robots or zombie
chickens; or if it makes your day to
learn that John Wayne's real first
name was Marion; or if you like film
genres such as The Five Best Romantic
Comedies Featuring Werewolves; or if
you know all the comebacks of at least
one film by heart...

...this book is for you!

Evolution of the Batman Costume

1943
Actors: Lewis Wilson and Robert Lowery
Style: practically cosplay, wrinkled overalls, floppy ears.

1989
Actor: Michael Keaton
Style: total leather, gothic but drooping shoulders.

1966
Actor: Adam West
Style: lycra pajamas, bikini undies, fatty bulges, painted-on eyebrows.

1995
Actor: Alfredo Casero
Style: No.

1995
Actor: Val Kilmer
Style: latex + iron-pumping thermoformed breastplate.

2005
Actor: Christian Bale
Style: austere, all-Kevlar, Supercop Special Forces genre but with a cape.

1997
Actor: George Clooney
Style: chrome finishing touches recalling drift style, prominent nipples in the first version.

Actors Who Never Got To Play Batman

Alec Baldwin — Too much hair gel.

Clint Eastwood — Too old.

David Boreanaz — Too vampirish.

Mel Gibson — Too Mel Gibson.

Tom Selleck — Too much mustache.

Charlie Sheen — Too crazy.

Johnny Depp — Too much of a wimp.

Bill Murray — No, seriously?

Actors Who Never Got To Play The Joker

Robin Williams

Adrien Brody

David Bowie

Pop Stars Miscast in Unsuitable Movie Roles

Ringo Starr in Son of Dracula
A musical comedy about vampires in which Ringo plays the role of Merlin the Magician.

Rihanna in Battleship
Featuring a full-blown naval battle against aliens who dread the Sun and yet choose to land in Hawaii.

Snoop Dogg in Starsky and Hutch
But it did suit him well, in fact.

Kylie Minogue in Street Fighter
Swept Jean-Claude Van Damme off his feet during filming. That's something!

Mick Jagger in Freejack
For the role of a hardened and ruthless mercenary from the future, you immediately think of Mick Jagger, right?

Iggy Pop in The Crow 2
Iggy plays the villain and had to go up against Bon Jovi in the role of the Crow.

Phil Collins in Hook
But hey, chill. He doesn't sing.

Jennifer Lopez in Anaconda
An R&B diva battles a giant reptile.

Who wants to play a Quebecois hockey player with a redneck mustache and big phallus?
Justin Timberlake in The Love Guru

All the Different Ways Robert De Niro Has Died

Animated Films Featuring Puppets:
Not Recommended for Younger Viewers

Dark Crystal By Jim Henson and Frank Oz.

Mystic prophecy, grand quests, planetary alignments, and lots of shaggy, beastly monsters. Visual poetry guaranteed, but for 10-year-olds or younger, nothing but nightmares.

"When the three suns are finally realigned
That which divided them shall be destroyed
Two will become one and one remain whole
By the hand of a Gelfling and none other."

Team America
By Trey Parker, Matt Stone and Pam Brady.

A very special take on happiness with puppets, paramilitaries, blood, sex, Kim Jong-il, profanity, and Sean Penn devoured by a panther.

There are three categories of people in the world: idiots, jerks and dickheads.

Meet the Feebles By Peter Jackson.

Exactly like the Muppet Show but with drugs, vomit and STDs.

"Do you really think people are interested in nasal sex?"

The Best Romantic Comedies without Hugh Grant

Pretty Woman
The only fairy tale where the princess wears thigh-high boots.

Valentine's Day
An ensemble cast in a world where everyone is very beautiful.

The Holiday
Are you coming on holiday? Yes, if Jude Law is there.

Crazy, Stupid, Love
Ryan Gosling as love coach? Yes, very well.

There's Something About Mary
Love mutilated by zipper.

Zack and Miri Make a Porno
Proof that romanticism and the *Star Wars* series are compatible.

Forgetting Sarah Marshall
Mila Kunis playing a hotel receptionist = science fiction.

Heartbreaker
Exclusion of foreign cultural influence.

He's Just Not That Into You
"If a guy doesn't call you, it's because he doesn't want to call you."

Inventions We'd Like To See in Real Life

The neuralyzer in Men in Black
To do illegal or disgusting things and afterwards wipe people's memory clean.

The transporter from Star Trek
Because no one likes the subway and also to be able to say: "Scotty, beam me up."

The electromagnetic shrinking machine in Honey, I Shrunk the Kids
If you are a parent, you already want it.

The Point of View Gun in The Hitchhiker's Guide to the Galaxy
Make your enemy adopt your point of view. Very useful in the context of marital life.

WONKA 3 COURSE DINNER CHEWING GUM

The Three-Course Dinner Chewing Gum in Charlie and the Chocolate Factory
PROS: Daily nourishment.
CONS: You change into a giant blueberry.

The memory-erasing machine in Eternal Sunshine of the Spotless Mind
When alcohol and chocolate are not enough.

The hoverboard in Back to the Future
And the self-lacing shoes, the auto-drying jacket, the pizza hydrator, and the Pepsi Perfect.

All the inventions in Wallace and Gromit
And especially the mechanical trousers.

The Scariest Houses

The Bates Motel in *Psycho*

Don't ask for the room with a shower.

The cabin in *The Cabin in the Woods*

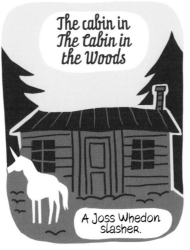

A Joss Whedon slasher.

The Dakota Building Apartments in *Rosemary's Baby*

Ask John Lennon.

The house in *The Amityville Horror*

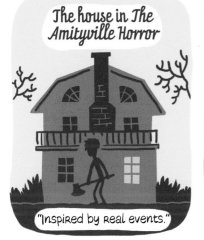

"Inspired by real events."

The Overlook Hotel in *The Shining*

Pleasant staff, children welcome.

Hannibal Lecter's cell in *The Silence of the Lambs*

Today's special is you.

The suburban house in *Poltergeist*

All creature comforts, veranda overlooking Hell.

The bedroom in *Paranormal Activity*

"Night 13: piercing screams, chandelier that moves by itself—nothing out of the ordinary."

The cabin in *The Evil Dead*

Here, the dead also have a right to live.

Hairstyles from the Beyond in Fantasy Films

Ewan McGregor in The Phantom Menace
Crewcut + rattail. A Padawan buzz.

Gary Oldman in The Fifth Element
Cyber-Nazi with a forelock.

John Travolta in Battlefield Earth
Dreadlocks come to outer space.

Chris Tucker in The Fifth Element
A banana-shaped blonde wig, if you can believe it.

Mel Gibson in Mad Max Beyond Thunderdome
Maybe the biggest mullet in the world.

Sean Connery in Zardoz
Disregard the underpants and thigh boots. Check out the hair. Yes, it's a braid.

David Bowie in Labyrinth
Sometimes words fail...

Johnny Depp in Charlie and the Chocolate Factory
A simple bob, Snow White style.

Wesley Snipes in Demolition Man
It'll be cool in 2032, trust me!

Gary Oldman in Dracula
Double buns?

Nicolas Cage's Hairstyles from the Beyond

Peggy Sue Got Married
A peroxide ducktail.

Raising Arizona
Unkempt + mustache.

Valley Girl
Teased and highlighted.

Face/Off
Very high forehead.

Kiss of Death
Widow's peak compensated by a goatee.

The Weather Man
A nice guy's hairstyle, but a lost soul.

Con Air
Manly extensions.

Vampire's Kiss
Blonde balayage.

Bangkok Dangerous
Medium length and balding.

Adaptation
Frizzy curls.

Ghost Rider
Firming gel wet look.

Season of the Witch
Magical hair plugs.

Michael Bay Movie Kits

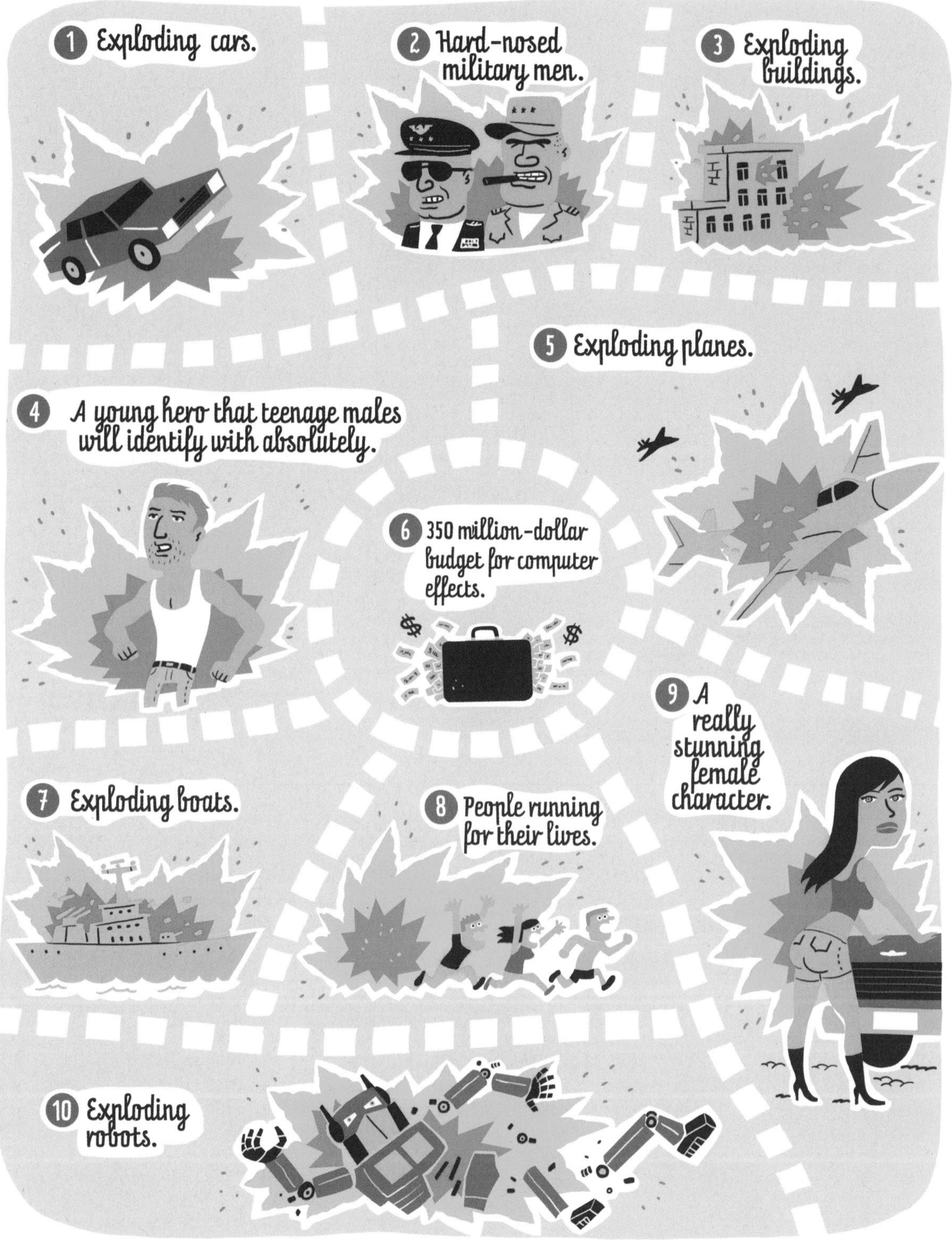
1 Exploding cars.
2 Hard-nosed military men.
3 Exploding buildings.
4 A young hero that teenage males will identify with absolutely.
5 Exploding planes.
6 350 million-dollar budget for computer effects.
$
$
7 Exploding boats.
8 People running for their lives.
9 A really stunning female character.
10 Exploding robots.

Actors considered for the role of Rambo before the choice fell on Sylvester Stallone

Clint Eastwood

Robert De Niro

Kris Kristofferson

Nick Nolte

Al Pacino

Steve McQueen

Paul Newman

Dustin Hoffman

John Travolta

Terence Hill

Goonies Wiki 1

Whatever became of them?

Jeff Cohen
a.k.a. Chunk, became a Hollywood lawyer.

Josh Brolin
a.k.a. Brand, starred in *No Country for Old Men* and played George Bush in Oliver Stone's *W*.

Martha Plimpton and Kerri Green
a.k.a. Stef and Andy, appeared in the series *ER*.

Corey Feldman
a.k.a. Mouth, was in *Stand by Me* and *The Lost Boys*. He voiced Donatello in *Teenage Mutant Ninja Turtles*.

Sean Astin
a.k.a. Mickey, was Samwise in *The Lord of the Rings*.

Jonathan Ke Quan
a.k.a. Data, played Short Round in *Indiana Jones and the Temple of Doom*. A Taekwondo expert, he did the fight choreography for *The One* and *X-Men*.

Cannon Beach
with its mysterious rock on the Oregon coast. It appears again in *1941*, *Point Break*, *Free Willy* and episode one of *Twilight*.

Goonies Wiki 2

Jonathan Ke Quan
promised his mother not to swear in the movie and that's why he spelled out "holy S-H-I-T" in the original version.

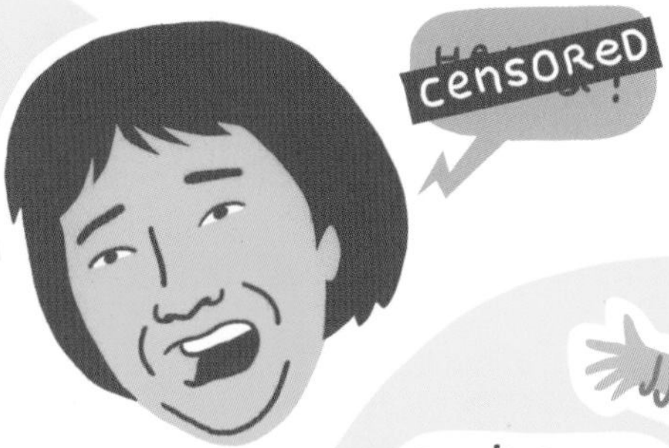
CENSORED

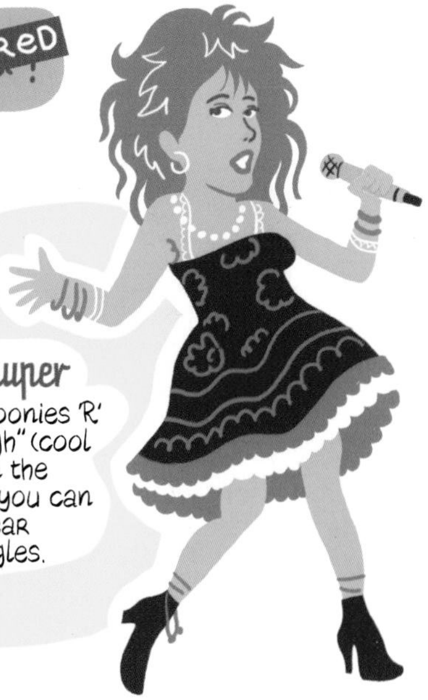

Cyndi Lauper
sang "The Goonies 'R' Good Enough" (cool video). In the soundtrack you can also hear The Bangles.

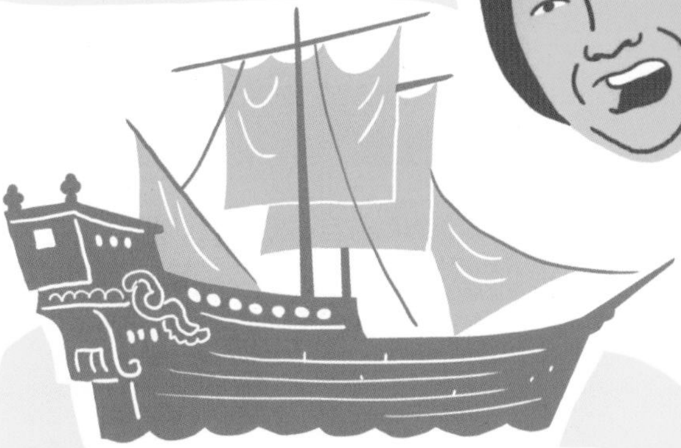

One-Eyed Willy's Pirate Ship
was built to full scale. After the film was finished, the production company wanted to donate it, but no one wanted it and so it was finally scrapped.

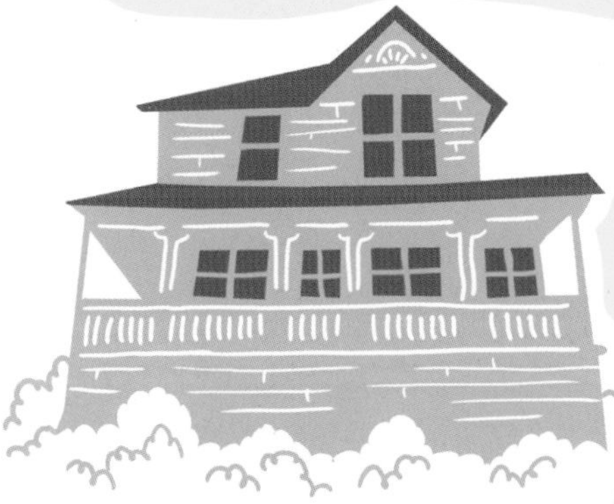

Walsh's House
is real. You'll find it at 368 38th St, Astoria, Oregon.

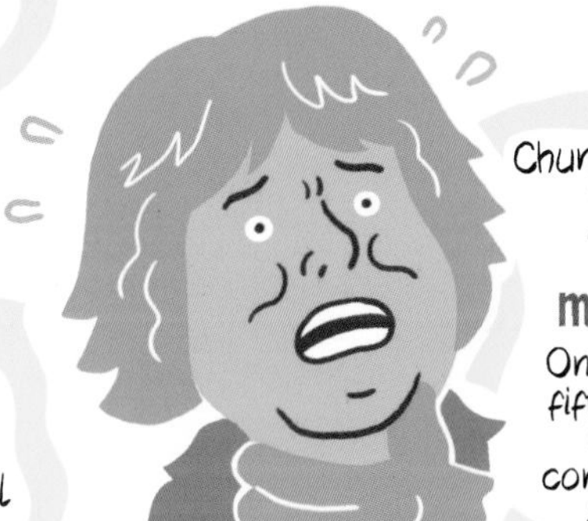

Chunk's Proustian moment:
Chunk's monologue
One minute and fifteen seconds of weeping confessions with fake vomit.

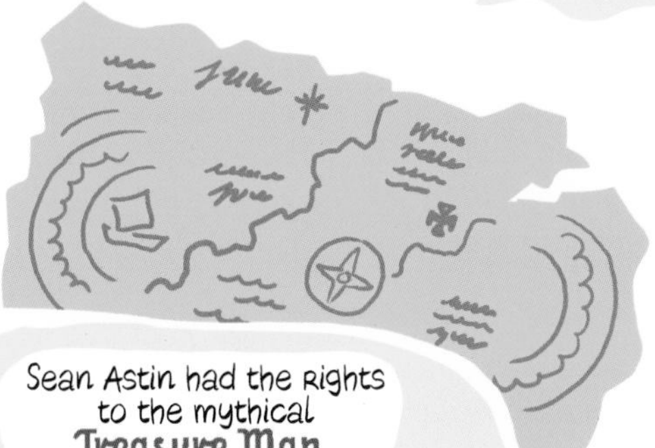

Sean Astin had the rights to the mythical
Treasure Map
at the end of filming. But his mother threw it away by mistake a few years later.

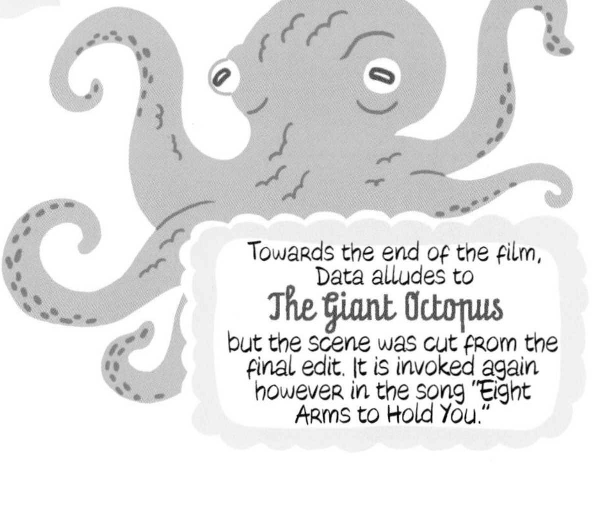

Towards the end of the film, Data alludes to
The Giant Octopus
but the scene was cut from the final edit. It is invoked again however in the song "Eight Arms to Hold You."

More or Less Credible Actors in the Role of a Robot

Haley Joel Osment in A.I. Artificial Intelligence
The child robot who says "Mama, I love you."

Jan Holm in Alien
A traitorous robot that ends up decapitated but actually had it coming.

Michael Fassbender in Prometheus
The robot so well-designed he seems to have emotions.

Jude Law in A.I. Artificial Intelligence
The gigolo robot who can dance like a god.

Yul Brynner in Westworld
This robot gunslinger takes his role to heart and guns down everyone in sight.

Rutger Hauer in Blade Runner
The cruel robot with the soul of a poet.

Robin Williams in Bicentennial Man
This all-plastic robot learns the most valuable lesson about love.

Kristanna Loken in Terminator 3
The top model robot who is cut in half without ruining her manicure.

More or Less Sexy Statue of Liberty Mishaps

Planet of the Apes
Buried in sand.

Escape From New York
Decapitated.

Superman 4
Carried aloft.

Ghostbusters
Possessed by good spirits.

Independence Day
Knocked over.

Deep Impact
Swept away by a tsunami.

Judge Dredd
Undergoes a craniotomy.

X-Men
Lasered in the face.

Batman Forever
Attacked by helicopter.

A.I. Artificial Intelligence
Sunk.

The Day After Tomorrow
Deep frozen.

Cloverfield
Decapitated again.

The Coen Brothers vs. The Wachowski Sisters

Michael Stuhlbarg in *A Serious Man*.	**Philosophic questions about the role of man in the world**	Keanu Reeves in *The Matrix*.
No, it's too expensive.	**Rotating camera shots around stationary actors**	*The Matrix*.
Billy <u>Bob</u> Thornton in *The Barber*.	**Principal character who dies in the end**	Keanu Reeves in *The Matrix Revolutions*.
The final battle with the Germans in *The Big Lebowski*.	**Combat scene with martial arts**	One out of every three scenes in *The Matrix*.
Javier Bardem in *No Country for Old Men*.	**Ruthless unstoppable killer**	Agent Smith in *The Matrix*.
John Goodman in *Barton Fink*	**Big fear-inspiring guy**	Laurence Fishburne in *The Matrix*.
Homer's Odyssey in *O Brother, Where Art Thou?*	**Mythological references**	Zion, a Rastafarian paradise in *The Matrix*.
Scarlett Johansson in *The Barber*.	**Actress radiating high-voltage sexuality**	Monica Bellucci in *The Matrix Reloaded*.
The CD in *Burn After Reading*.	**Mysterious digital file at the center of the intrigue**	The Matrix in *The Matrix*.
True Grit.	**Nerve-shattering shootouts**	*The Matrix*.
Justin Timberlake in *Inside Llewyn Davis*.	**Original band with stars playing**	Massive Attack in *The Matrix*.
No, but they bumped into each other once, at Cannes.	**Lambert Wilson's presence**	*The Matrix* and *The Matrix Reloaded*.

In what movie do these objects appear?

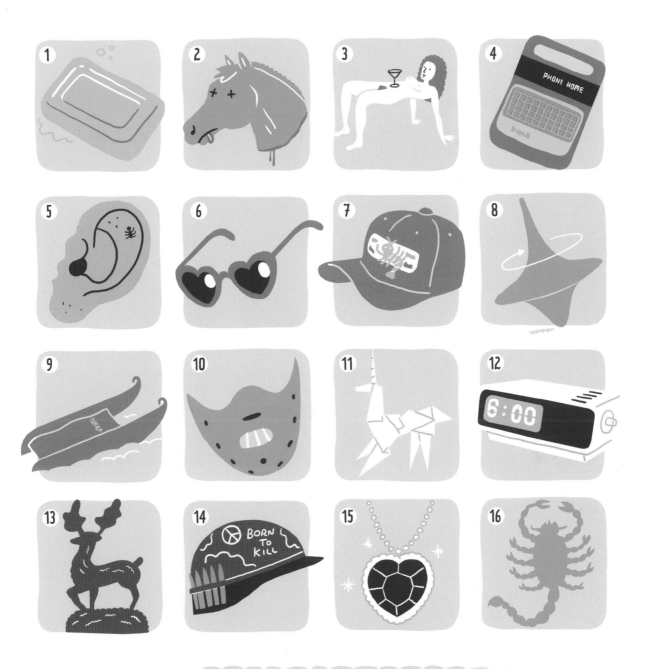

The Most Macho Comebacks
by Arnold Schwarzenegger

I'll be back.

Terminator 2

Come with me if you want to live.

Hasta la vista, baby.

It's a beautiful day and we're out killing drug dealers. Are there any in the house?

Last Action Hero

How exactly are you going to snap your fingers, after I rip off both of your thumbs?

If it bleeds, we can kill it.

You're one... *ugly* motherfucker!

Predator

Conan the Barbarian

To crush your enemies, to see them driven before you, and to hear the lamentations of their women.

Terminator

First I'm going to use you as a human shield. Then I'm going to kill this guard over here with the Patterson trocar on the table. And then I was thinking about breaking your neck.

Commando

Consider that a divorce!

Eraser

Total Recall

You're a funny guy, Sully, I like you. That's why I'm going to kill you last.

The next time, you're dead. And that only happens once.

True Lies

Adam and Evil!

Batman and Robin

Red Heat

You deal drugs in my country and one fine morning when you wake up, boom! You find your balls in the water glass on your night table.

I suppose nothing hurts you. ~ Only pain.

Conan the Destroyer

Actors who have fallen in love on set

Tom Cruise & Nicole Kidman
Movie: *Days of Thunder.*

Johnny Depp & Winona Ryder
Movie: *Edward Scissorhands.*

Jude Law & Sienna Miller
Movie: *Alphie.*

Uma Thurman & Ethan Hawke
Movie: *Gattaca.*

Kristen Stewart & Robert Pattinson
Movie: *Twilight.*

Julia Roberts & Kiefer Sutherland
Movie: *Flatliners.*

Taylor Lautner & Taylor Swift
Movie: *Valentine's Day.*

Kim Basinger & Prince
Movie: *Batman.*

Meg Ryan & Russell Crowe
Movie: *Proof of Life.*

Richard Burton & Elizabeth Taylor
Movie: *Cleopatra.*

Warren Beatty & Madonna
Movie: *Dick Tracy.*

Angelina Jolie & Brad Pitt
Movie: *Mr. & Mrs. Smith.*

In What Films Do We See The Actor's Buttocks?

Sylvester Stallone

in *First Blood.*

Michael Fassbender

in *Shame.*

Bruce Willis and Brad Pitt

in *12 Monkeys.*

Kevin Costner

in *Dances with Wolves.*

Shia LaBeouf

in *Nymphomaniac.*

Ewan McGregor

in *Young Adam. And in plenty more films.*

Justin Timberlake

in *Friends with Benefits.*

Richard Gere

in *American Gigolo.*

Christian Bale

in *American Psycho.*

Colin Farrell

in *Alexander.*

Arnold Schwarzenegger

in *Terminator 1.*

Leonardo DiCaprio

in *Total Eclipse.*

In What Films Do We See The Actress's Breasts?

Uma
Thurman
in Dangerous
Liaisons.

Eva
Green
in
Perfect Sense.

Marion Cotillard
in
Pretty Things.

Monica
Bellucci
in
Dracula.

Halle
Berry
in
Swordfish.

Angelina
Jolie
in
Foxfire, Gia...
And plenty
of other films.

Gwyneth
Paltrow
in
Shakespeare
in Love.

Penélope Cruz
in
Open Your Eyes.

Nicole
Kidman
in
Billy
Bathgate.

Anne
Hathaway
in
Love &
Other Drugs.

Demi Moore
in
Striptease.

Madonna
in
Body of Evidence.

Weird Movies with Implausible Plots

 The Curse of the Cat People 1944

 CAT-WOMEN OF THE MOON 1953

 SANTA CLAUS conquers THE MARTIANS 1964

MY MOM'S a WERE-WOLF 1989

 Emmanuelle and the Last Cannibals 1978

 SuperStooges vs. the WONDER WOMEN 1975

 Killer Klowns from Outer Space 1988

the Adventures of Shark Boy & Lava Girl 3-D 2004

SURF NAZIS MUST DIE 1987

LOBSTER MAN FROM MARS 1989

 Teenage Cat girls in Heat 1993

 A nymphoid BARBARIAN in DINOSAUR HELL 1990

 Bikini Girls on Dinosaur Planet 2005

KISS ME QUICK! 1964

the ATTACK OF THE GIANT MOUSSAKA 1999

28

Marlon Brando's Flowchart

Superman's father in *Superman*.

Mexican revolutionary in *Viva Zapata !*

Roman general in *Julius Caesar*.

Mafia patriarch in *The Godfather*.

A mad scientist in *The Island of Dr. Moreau*.

U.S. Army Colonel in *Apocalypse Now*.

New Age guru in *Candy*.

Sheriff in *The Chase*.

Nazi officer in *The Young Lions*.

Film producer in *The Brave*.

Mutineer leader in *Mutiny on the Bounty*.

Motorcycle gang leader in *The Wild One*.

Dockworker in *On the Waterfront*.

Blue-collar worker in *A Streetcar Named Desire*.

A guitar-playing drifter in *The Fugitive Kind*.

Alien, as told by Ethel (6½ years old)

 So there's this space ship with some nice men and a pretty lady inside. And there's also a small kitty cat.

 They land on this really ugly planet where there's just rocks, wind and fog.

It's a bit like the Oregon coast. I went there once with mommy.

 As the guys are walking around this planet, they find some big eggs, like Easter eggs, you know, but more sticky.

 It turns out there are these monsters inside the eggs who attack this one guy. Like Rotten Kinder Surprise chocolates, you know.

He should have been more careful.

 Then the man gets all sick.

One day at school, my friend Bobby got sick to his stomach like what happened to the guy, you know. Except that he vomited on Victoria.

Nicely done, if you ask me. I don't like Victoria.

Then there are these baby monsters who come out of the guys and get big real fast.

I had a hamster once that grew big like that, but I don't think the monsters in the movie are like hamsters.

 Actually, we don't see what's happening a lot of the time because it's all dark. The people who made the movie must have run out of light bulbs.

 My favorite movie is *Finding Nemo*.

This one is good too but I think there aren't enough songs.

 After that, I had to cover my eyes because I was afraid for the little kitty cat.

 But when I covered my eyes, I sort of fell asleep a little bit.

 When I woke up, the lady had a thing that shot out flames to kill the monster. It was really neat!

 Then all the guys died, but luckily the kitty cat was okay, phew!

 I can't tell you more about the movie cause then mommy came in and turned the TV off.

And then she told daddy he was a ~~total dickhead~~ a jerk for leaving his DVDs lying around everywhere. And he shouldn't be surprised if I am going to need psychoanalysis.

The Rules of Fight Club

1 You do not talk about Fight Club.

2 You do not talk about Fight Club.

3 Someone yells stop, goes limp, taps out, the fight is over.

4 Only two guys to a fight.

5 One fight at a time.

6 No shirts, no shoes.

7 Fights will go on as long as they have to.

8 If this is your first night at Fight Club, you __have__ to fight.

 "It's only after we've lost everything that we're free to do anything."

"On a long enough timeline, the survival rate for everyone drops to zero."

Movies That Aren't Interesting If You Know The Ending

Planet of the Apes
It turns out it's Planet Earth.

The Sixth Sense
It turns out Bruce Willis is a ghost but doesn't know it.

The Others
It turns out Nicole Kidman is a ghost but doesn't know it.

Psycho
It turns out Anthony Perkins thinks he's his dead mother.

The Game
It turns out it's all a game.

The Village
It turns out it's a nature reserve for old hippies.

Dark City
It turns out the city is an experience conjured up by extraterrestrials.

Vanilla Sky
It turns out nothing exists and Tom Cruise is dead.

Memento
It turns out Guy Pearce is lying to himself.

Or maybe not...

Fight Club
It turns out Tyler exists only in the mind of the narrator.

Usual Suspects
It turns out Keyser Söze is Kevin Spacey.

6.0

5.6

5.0

2001: A Space Odyssey
It turns out nothing makes sense in the end.

Things We Can't See in American Movies Because of the Hays Code

(A set of industry moral guidelines in effect from 1934 to 1966.)

Vengeance

(Except in historical films.)

Drug dealing

Nudity

Excessive or lascivious kissing

Prostitution

White slaves

(Black slaves, okay.)

Homosexuality

Alcohol consumption

(Unless absolutely necessary to the plot.)

Profanity invoking God and religion

Childbirth

(Even in silhouette.)

Intimate relations between people of different races

Excessively suggestive dancing

Article 9: "The treatment of bedrooms must be governed by good taste and delicacy."

Superhero Film Adaptations
We Could Perhaps Have Done Without

Captain America
1979.
Sometimes blue pajamas and a motorcycle helmet aren't enough.

Supergirl
1984.
'Cause a short skirt and ankle boots lack superhero credibility.

Superman 4
1987.
'Cause the special effects make your eyes bleed.

Batman & Robin
1997.
'Cause even the actors seem embarrassed.

3 Giant Men
(aka: Captain America & Santo vs. Spider-Man)
1973.
Turkish version with a Mexican wrestler. Captain America is really out of luck when it comes to the movies.

The Fantastic Four
1994.
'Cause the movie was cobbled together too fast, just so the studio would not lose its rights.

Indian Superman
(Dariya Dil)
1988.
'Cause no one wants to see Superman singing in a family drama.

Catwoman
2004.
'Cause... well, okay, Halle Berry is stunning, but that doesn't make it right.

The Spirit
2008.
'Cause even Samuel L. Jackson is lousy in this.

Unknown Actors Who Nonetheless Played Legendary Characters 1

Doug Bradley
Pinhead in Hellraiser.

John Matuszak
Sloth in The Goonies. (Former American football champion).

Michael J. Anderson
The little man in red in Twin Peaks: Fire Walk with Me.

Haruo Nakajima
Godzilla and many more Japanese latex monsters for 23 years.

David Prowse
Darth Vader in Star Wars, Episodes 4, 5 and 6. (Also a champion English weightlifter in 1962).

Peter Mayhew
Chewbacca in Star Wars, Episodes 3, 4, 5, 6, and 7.

Unknown Actors Who Nonetheless Played Legendary Characters 2

Bolaji Badejo

The alien in *Alien*.

Ray Park

Darth Maul in *Star Wars, Episode 1* (Wushu world champion, a Chinese martial art).

Anthony Daniels

C-3PO in all seven episodes of *Star Wars*.

Kenny Baker

R2-D2 in all six original episodes of *Star Wars*.

Tim Curry

Pennywise the clown in *It*. (He also played the main character in *The Rocky Horror Picture Show*).

Kevin Peter Hall

The Predator in *The Predator*. (He also played Bigfoot in *Harry and the Hendersons*).

Movies It's Hard To Believe Ever Saw the Light of Day

Popeye
1980.
With Robin Williams who is beyond all that now.

Super Mario Bros.
1993.
With Bob Hoskins and Dennis Hopper miscast in the role of Koopa.

Dragon Ball Z
1991.
There is a 2009 version with Chow Yun-fat as Turtle Hermit.

The Wiz
1978.
The Wizard of Oz meets Harlem, with Diana Ross as Dorothy and Michael Jackson as the scarecrow who scares little children.

Howard the Duck
1986.
A duck from outer space with a foul mouth. Produced by George Lucas, feeling a bit lost after Star Wars.

Terminus
1987.
A French version of Mad Max with Johnny Hallyday as the hero.

Thunderbirds
2004.
An adaptation of a '60s TV series with real actors instead of puppets. What a great idea!

Inspector Gadget
1999.
With Matthew "Go, Go, Gadget" Broderick.

Masters of the Universe
1987.
With Dolph Lundgren in his underwear in the role of He-Man.

The Gaul
2001.
A wig with Christopher Lambert underneath.

Movies on Tight Budgets That Made a Lot of Money with Unknown Actors

💼 = Budget 💵 = Box Office ★ = Profit Return

Eraserhead
💼 $100,000
💵 $7 million
★ × 70

Friday the 13th

💼 $550,000
💵 $59 million
★ × 107

Clerks
💼 $27,000
💵 $3.9 million
★ × 144

Halloween

💼 $300,000
💵 $60 million
★ × 200

Mad Max 1

💼 $400,000
💵 $99 million
★ × 247

The Night of the Living Dead

💼 $114,000
💵 $30 million
★ × 263

Deep Throat

💼 $25,000
💵 $30 million
★ × 1 200

The Blair Witch Project

💼 $50,000
💵 $248 million
★ × 4 960

Paranormal Activity

💼 $15,000
💵 $193 million
★ × 12 866

For comparison purposes, each minute of Titanic cost $1.4 million.

A Comparison of
Jean-Claude Van Damme and Chuck Norris

Jean-Claude Van Damme		Chuck Norris
Jean-Claude Camille François Van Varenberg.	**Real Name**	Carlos Ray Norris.
European Light Contact Kickboxing Champion.	**Sports Rankings**	World Professional Middleweight Karate Champion.
Can do the splits thanks to five years of classic dance.	**Talents**	Could transform into an eagle and a bear in Forest Warrior.
Created a clothing line.	**Weaknesses**	Played in Top Dog.
"Life belongs to all the living. It's both a dream and a feeling."	**Philosophy**	Writes about Western Christianity.
Unknown.	**Political Convictions**	Right-wing Republican.
The Muscles from Brussels.	**Nickname**	No one gives Chuck Norris a nickname.
5' 8"	**Height**	5' 8½"
Himself in JCVD (A film about him.)	**Best Role**	Himself in Sidekicks.

Unbearable Characters Who We'd Like To See Dead by the End of the Film

1 Jar Jar Binks in *Star Wars Episode 1: The Phantom Menace.*

2 Jar Jar Binks in *Star Wars Episode 2: Attack of the Clones.*

3 Jar Jar Binks in *Star Wars Episode 3: Revenge of the Sith.*

Special mention **goes to Scarlett O'Hara in** *Gone with the Wind.*

Tim Burton Movie Kit

1 *Johnny Depp*

Vampire Movie Titles
We Actually Like

BILLY THE KID VS. DRACULA
1966

 Guess What Happened to COUNT DRACULA?
1971

BLACULA
1972

 Dracula in Pakistan
1967

 DRACULA'S DOG
1978

 LOVE AT FIRST BITE
1978

 SAMURAI VAMPIRE BIKERS FROM HELL
1992

I Bought a Vampire Motorcycle
1990

Killer BARBYS vs. DRACULA
2002

JESUS CHRIST Vampire Hunter
2001

 ROBO VAMPIRE
1998

Vampire Killers
2009

SPERMULA
1976

 BONNIE & CLYDE VS. DRACULA
2008

 Vampires Suck
2010

Are You
Shorter or Taller Than...

Danny DeVito — 4' 11"

Michael J. Fox — 5' 4"

Daniel Radcliffe — 5' 5"

Elijah Wood — 5' 6"

Tom Cruise — 5' 7"

Bruce Lee — 5' 7"

Jackie Chan — 5' 9"

Robert Downey Jr. — 5' 9"

Sylvester Stallone — 5' 10"

Daniel Craig — 5' 10"

Bruce Willis — 6' 0"

Morgan Freeman — 6' 2"

Clint Eastwood — 6' 5"

Christopher Lee — 6' 6"

Richard Kiel — 7' 2"

Are You
Shorter or Taller Than...

Carrie Fisher — 5' 1"

Salma Hayek — 5' 2"

Natalie Portman — 5' 3"

Jodie Foster — 5' 3"

Penelope Cruz — 5' 5"

Whoopi Goldberg — 5' 5"

Jessica Alba — 5' 7"

Kirsten Dunst — 5' 7"

Sandra Bullock — 5' 7"

Sharon Stone — 5' 9"

Gwyneth Paltrow — 5' 9"

Nicole Kidman — 5' 11"

Uma Thurman — 5' 11"

Sigourney Weaver — 6' 1"

Brigitte Nielsen — 6' 2"

Mischievous Objects That Kill People

A laundry-folding machine
The Mangler
1995

An elevator
The Lift
1983

A tire
Rubber
2010

A videotape
The Ring 2002

A wig
Scary Hair
2006

A vending machine
(and also a truck, a bridge...)
Maximum Overdrive
1986

A snowman
Jack Frost
1998

A fridge
The Refrigerator
1991

A bed
Death Bed: The
Bed That Eats
1977

+ all objects in Final Destination

46

The Evolution of Robin Hood's Attire

1938
Errol Flynn in *The Adventures of Robin Hood*. Form-hugging tights.

1969
Ralph Jenkins in *The Erotic Adventures of Robin Hood*. Bleach blond, casual outfit.

1976
Sean Connery in *Robin and Marian*. Balding, bearded, and loose clothing. Flower-child look.

1981
John Cleese in *Time Bandits*. Feathered hat, shirt by BHL, Snow White hairstyle.

1991
Kevin Costner in *Robin Hood: Prince of Thieves*. Mullet cut, tagelmust to look cool, leather and studs.

2001
Keira Knightley in *Princess of Thieves*. Plays Robin Hood's daughter who takes over from her aging father. Carefully disheveled hair, long dress.

2010
Russell Crowe in *Robin Hood*. Weather-beaten, cropped hair, postmodern sobriety.

Jackie Chan's Injuries
in the Course of Filming 120 Movies

(A non-exhaustive list)

Arm gashed by a sword
Snake in the Eagle's Shadow.

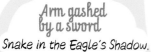

Broken nose (3 times)
In MR. NICE GUY, The Young Master and PROJECT A.

Dislocated sternum, resulting from a fall
ARMOUR OF GOD II.

Knocked out tooth
Snake in the Eagle's Shadow.

Legs crushed between two cars
Crime story.

Fractured vertebrae and dislocated pelvis
In Police Story resulting from a 50 ft. sliding fall.

Shattered vertebrae
In Police Story 3 after being clipped by a helicopter in flight.

Chin injury
Dragon Lord.

Skull fracture
After falling onto rocks in ARMOUR of God.

Dislocated knee
Falling off a skateboard in City Hunter.

Broken right ankle
Jumping into a hovercraft in Rumble in the Bronx.

Fingers lacerated by a snowboard
Police Story 4.

Actors Who Showed Poor Judgment in Declining Iconic Roles

Tom Selleck

did not play *Indiana Jones* because he was too busy filming *Magnum, P.I.*

Burt Reynolds

refused the role of Han Solo in *Star Wars*. He still regrets it.

Will Smith

didn't want to play Neo in *The Matrix*, because "the script was too complicated."

John Travolta

refused to play *Forrest Gump*. That would've been something to see.

You probably don't know who

Molly Ringwald

is, but you would if she hadn't refused to star in both *Pretty Woman* and *Ghost*.

Keanu Reeves

didn't want to be the hero in *Platoon* because there was too much violence. That's cute.

Jim Carrey

turned down the role of *Edward Scissorhands*. Oops!

Al Pacino

claims to have refused roles in *Pretty Woman*, *Die Hard* and *Star Wars*, but he is perhaps padding the truth a bit.

Sean Connery

refused the 10 million dollars he was offered to play Gandalf in *The Lord of the Rings*...

...because even after reading the books, he still didn't understand the story.

Actors Who've Played Gods in the Movies

▭▭▭▭ = Credibility Level

Morgan Freeman
God in *Bruce Almighty*.

Ursula Andress
Aphrodite in *Clash of the Titans*.

Sean Bean
Zeus in *Percy Jackson & the Olympians: The Lightning Thief*.

Liam Neeson
Zeus in *Wrath of the Titans*.

Hulk Hogan
Zeus in *Little Hercules in 3-D*.

Alanis Morissette
God in *Dogma*.

Anthony Hopkins
Odin in *Thor*.

Uma Thurman
Venus in *The Adventures of Baron Munchausen*.

Whoopi Goldberg
God in *It's a Very Merry Muppet Christmas Movie*.

Actors Who Have Played Satan in the Movies

= Fear Factor

Harvey Keitel

in *Little Nicky*. With horns and a pitchfork.

Robert De Niro

in *Angel Heart*. Suave. Can make his eyes glow.

Viggo Mortensen

in *The Prophecy*. Vicious and scary, and a little nasty.

Al Pacino

in *The Devil's Advocate*. A lawyer.

Elizabeth Hurley

in *Bedazzled*. Much to be said for her assets.

Jeff Goldblum

in *Mister Frost*. Total psychopath.

Jack Nicholson

in *The Witches of Eastwick*. Very raunchy.

Billy Crystal

in *Deconstructing Harry*. Cool.

Who Are These Evil Extraterrestrials?

Who Are These Nice Extraterrestrials?

10 : T.J. Newton (David Bowie) in *The Man Who Fell to Earth*.
9 : The little ETs who like synth music in *Close Encounters of the Third Kind*.
8 : Beldar (Dan Aykroyd) in *Coneheads*. - 7 : Pypar, the birdman in *Barbarella*.
6 : Mac (Jeff Goldblum) in *Earth Girls Are Easy.*
4 : The water alien in *The Abyss*. - 5 : Paul in *Paul.* -
1 : Frank in *Men in Black.* - 2 : Starman (Jeff Bridges) in *Starman.* - 3 : Christopher Johnson, the shrimp, in *District 9.*

If Quentin Tarantino Did a Remake of Jaws

Begin: A young woman in shorts dancing on the beach who then goes swimming and loses an arm to a shark. All that against the backdrop of '60s music.

She survives and gets an Amity Island cop to kill the shark. They talk and talk, and talk, for 16 minutes in the car.

The cop tries to convince the mayor to ban swimming on the beach. He doesn't listen, so the cop kills him with a baseball bat.

After that, he hires an old fisherman to help find the shark. The cop offers him a suitcase full of cash and they go to eat hamburgers.

And then they stop at a bar and dance to '60s music.

The next day, they set out by boat to look for the shark. But the shark seizes the old fisherman and tortures him for a long time by eating him in little bites.

Before dying, the fisherman gives his samurai sword to the cop so he can kill the beast.

The cop finds the shark. They talk for 16 minutes before facing off in a duel. Finally, the cop blows up the shark with a tank of compressed air.

The cop has bits and pieces of the shark and blood all over him. He lights up a cigarette and listens to '60s music on the boat radio.

The Best Lines by Crazy Characters

Choose Life. Choose a job. Choose a career...

Rent Boy in Trainspotting

And you will know I am the LORD when I lay my vengeance upon you.

Jules in Pulp Fiction

I ate his liver with some fava beans and a nice chianti...

Hannibal Lecter in Silence of the Lambs

You talkin' to me?

Travis in Taxi Driver

Stop, Dave. I'm afraid.

Hal 9000 in 2001: A Space Odyssey

HORROR has a face...

Colonel Kurtz in Apocalypse Now

Dr. Evil in Austin Powers
(the therapy scene)

When I was insolent, I was placed in a burlap bag and beaten with reeds...

The Vampire's Physical Evolution

Ugly and scary

Nosferatu (1922)

Sleek and well-dressed, version 1

Dracula (1931)

Sleek and well-dressed, version 2

Dracula (1958)

The femme fatale

Plan 9 from Outer Space (1959)

A shaggy Mexican who looks like nothing on Earth

The Brainiac (1962)

A buxom vampire

The Fearless Vampire Killers (1967)

A black vampire

Blacula (1972)

A Japanese vampire

Evil of Dracula (1974)

"Beautiful People" vampires

The Hunger (1983)

A nude vampire from outer space

Lifeforce (1985)

A bad-boy vampire

The Lost Boys (1987)

A vampire aesthete, sexy and very decadent

Interview with the Vampire (1994)

A super-buxom vampire

From Dusk till Dawn (1996)

A superhero vampire

Blade (1998)

A vampire who sparkles in the sun

Twilight (2008)

A vampire who writes a girlie blog

Vampire Academy (2014)

Actors Who Were Smart to Take On a Screen Name

Carlos Irwin Estevez

Charlie Sheen

Jennifer Linn Anastassakis

Jennifer Aniston

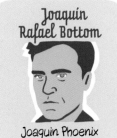

Joaquin Rafael Bottom

Joaquin Phoenix

Margaret Mary Emily Anne Hyra

Meg Ryan

Demetria Gene Guynes

Demi Moore

Allen Stewart Königsberg

Woody Allen

Nicholas Kim Coppola

Nicolas Cage

Krishna Pandit Bhanji

Ben Kingsley

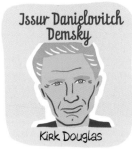

Michael Douglas

Michael Keaton

Issur Danielovitch Demsky

Kirk Douglas

Marion Robert Morrison

John Wayne

Archibald Alexander Leach

Cary Grant

* actors with unlikely middle names:

Thomas Cruise Mapother IV

Mel Columcille Gerard Gibson

Hugh John Mungo Grant

* A director who needs to take on a pseudonym if he hopes to succeed in Hollywood:

Apichatpong Weerasethakul

57

Who Are These Robots?

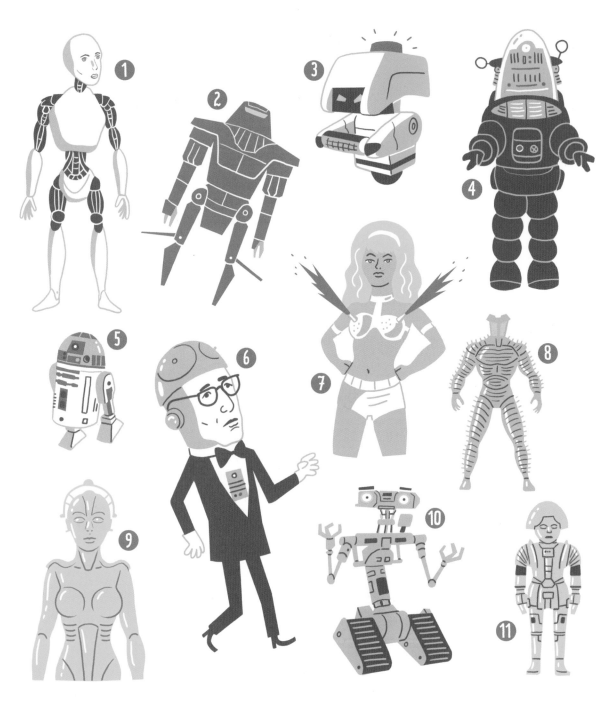

1: Sonny in *I, Robot*. - 2: Maximilian in *The Black Hole*. - 3: M-O the Cleaning Robot in *Wall-E*.
4: Robby in *Forbidden Planet*. - 5: R2-M5 in *The Phantom Menace* (ha, ha, gotcha!)
6: The fake Robot in *Sleeper*. - 7: A Fembot in *Austin Powers*.
8: The Destroyer in *Thor*. - 9: Maria in *Metropolis*. - 10: Johnny 5 in *Short Circuit*.
11: Twiki in *Buck Rogers in the 25th Century*.

What Are These Spaceships?

1 : The Nostromo in *Alien*. - 2 : Eagle 5 in *Spaceballs*.
3 : ET's spaceship in *E.T. the Extra-Terrestrial*. - 4 : Klingon Bird-of-Prey in *Star Trek III*.
5 : Discovery One in *2001: A Space Odyssey*. - 6 : Dave (Eddie Murphy) in *Meet Dave*. - 7 : A Heighliner in *Dune*.
8 : The Borg Cube in *Star Trek: First Contact*. - 9 : Boba Fett's Slave 1 in *The Empire Strikes Back*.
10 : A Martian flying saucer in *Mars Attacks!*

Actors Who Might've Played James Bond, But... No

Rejects:

Mel Gibson

Not English enough.

Christopher Lambert

Too Tarzan.

Eric Braeden

(Victor Newman in *The Young and the Restless*). Too mustached.

Sean Bean

He finally got a role as the villain.

Lambert Wilson

Too Frenchy.

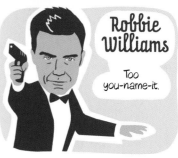

Robbie Williams

Too you-name-it.

Refused the role:

Cary Grant

Felt he was too old.

Clint Eastwood

Thought that the only real James Bond is Sean Connery.

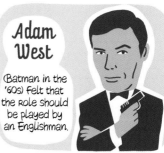

Adam West

(Batman in the '60s) felt that the role should be played by an Englishman.

Burt Reynolds

Also felt the role should be played by an Englishman.

Hugh Jackman

Was afraid of ruining his career.

Ewan McGregor

Also was afraid of ruining his career.

Costumes the Creators Should Have Been Sued For

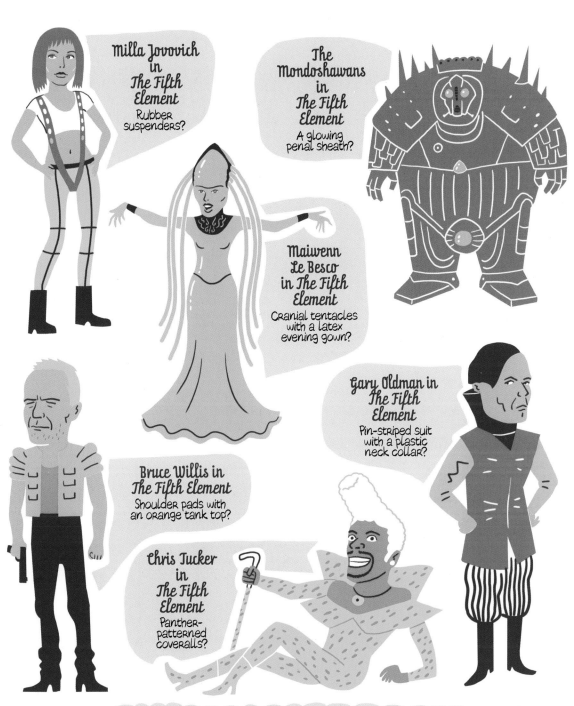

Milla Jovovich in *The Fifth Element*
Rubber suspenders?

The Mondoshawans in *The Fifth Element*
A glowing penal sheath?

Maiwenn Le Besco in *The Fifth Element*
Cranial tentacles with a latex evening gown?

Gary Oldman in *The Fifth Element*
Pin-striped suit with a plastic neck collar?

Bruce Willis in *The Fifth Element*
Shoulder pads with an orange tank top?

Chris Tucker in *The Fifth Element*
Panther-patterned coveralls?

To round out the list, we'd also mention Sean Connery in *Zardoz*, Arnold Schwarzenegger in *The Running Man*, and all the costumes in *Barbarella*.

Quebecois Translations of English Movie Titles

(The Charter of the French Language, in force in Quebec, strongly encourages distributors to translate English titles.)

Ça va Clancher!
Speed 2

POULETS en FUITE
Chicken Run

Tuer Bill
Kill Bill

Folies de Graduation
American Pie

L'amour est un Pouvoir sacré
Breaking the Waves

FERROVIPATHES
Trainspotting

DU SOLEIL PLEIN LA TÊTE ☀
Eternal Sunshine of the Spotless Mind

Danse Lascive
Dirty Dancing

MON FANTÔME D'AMOUR
Ghost

L'INCONNU DE LAS VEGAS
Ocean's Eleven

Fiction pulpeuse
Pulp Fiction

LE BAGARREUR DE RUE
Street Fighter

RAPIDES ET DANGEREUX
Fast and Furious

SEPT
Seven

A Tally of James Bond Mission Kills

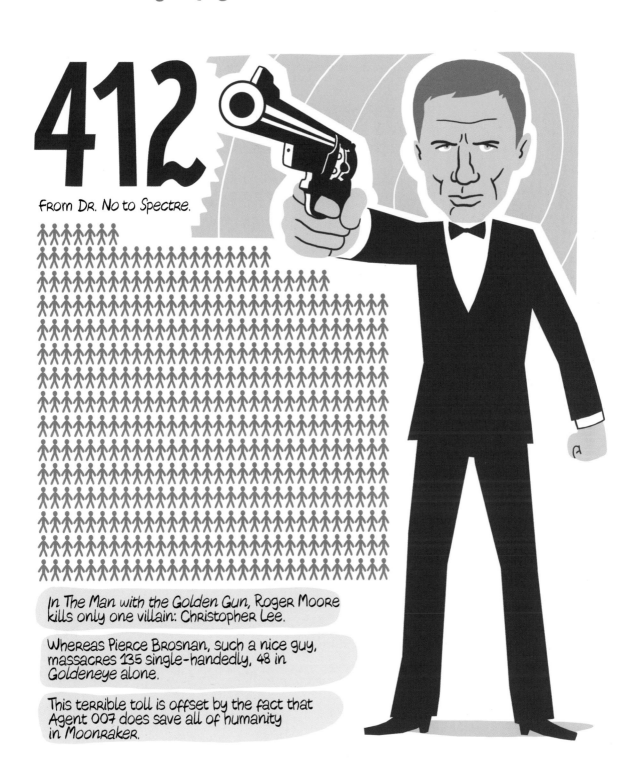

412

From *Dr. No* to *Spectre*.

In *The Man with the Golden Gun*, Roger Moore kills only one villain: Christopher Lee.

Whereas Pierce Brosnan, such a nice guy, massacres 135 single-handedly, 48 in *Goldeneye* alone.

This terrible toll is offset by the fact that Agent 007 does save all of humanity in *Moonraker*.

Michel Gondry Movie Kit

Interesting Facts About The Lord of the Rings

Viggo Mortensen

stated that to immerse himself in the role, he slept with his sword throughout the filming.

The Fearsome Screeching of the Nazguls

was mixed from the screams of Fran Walsh, Peter Jackson's wife.

The Giant Spider's Scream

came from a young Tasmanian devil.

159 Prosthetic Noses

were created for Ian McKellen, who played Gandalf.

20,000 Extras

were used in the filming.

2.9 Billion Dollars

was the trilogy's total cost, a little more than the GDP of Modavia.

1,600 Pair of Feet

were made out of latex for the Hobbits.

If Viggo

seemed convincing when he cried out in rage and fell to his knees after kicking a Uruk-hai helmet, it wasn't so much because he is a good actor as the fact that he actually broke a toe.

Christopher Lee

said he reread The Lord of the Rings every year since it was published in 1954.

Children Who Inspire the Most Fear

Uneasy

The white-haired children with glowing eyes
Village of the Damned
Conceived by aliens.

Damien
The Omen
Cute and well-mannered, but actually the antichrist.

Disturbing

Mitsuko
Dark Water (2002)
The cause of all the water damage.

Freaky

The Murdered Twins
The Shining
Blue dresses and signs of axe wounds.

Terrifying

The Ghost of the Dead Young Girl
The Sixth Sense
A sweetheart, but vomits strange stuff.

Beyond words

Young Regan
The Exorcist
Can swivel her head 360 degrees and is quite profane.

Macaulay Culkin
Home Alone.

Just How Big Are Those Giant Monsters?

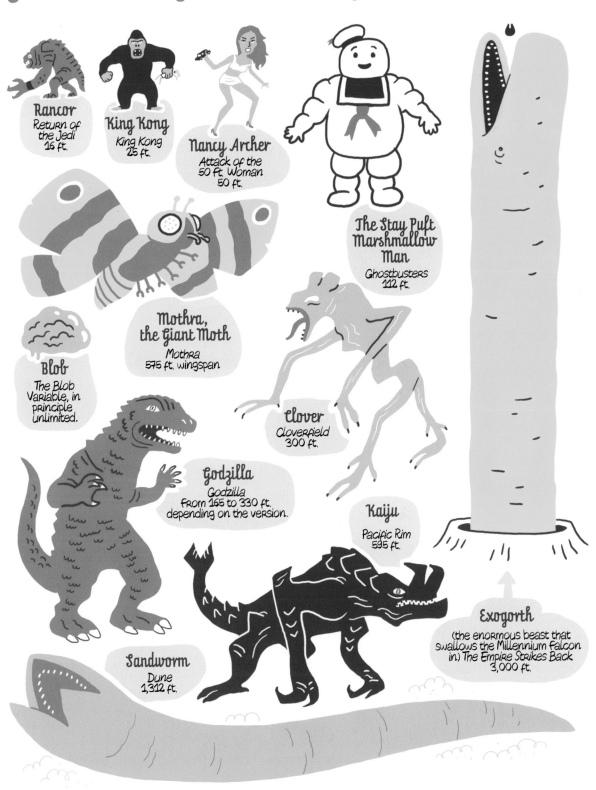

Rancor
Return of the Jedi
16 ft.

King Kong
King Kong
25 ft.

Nancy Archer
Attack of the 50 ft. Woman
50 ft.

The Stay Puft Marshmallow Man
Ghostbusters
112 ft.

Mothra, the Giant Moth
Mothra
575 ft. wingspan

Blob
The Blob
Variable, in principle unlimited.

Clover
Cloverfield
300 ft.

Godzilla
Godzilla
from 165 to 330 ft. depending on the version.

Kaiju
Pacific Rim
595 ft.

Exogorth
(the enormous beast that swallows the Millennium Falcon in) The Empire Strikes Back
3,000 ft.

Sandworm
Dune
1,312 ft.

Awful Feature-Length Movies That the Actors Would Prefer Erased from the Record

Arnold Schwarzenegger in *Hercules in New York*

Leonardo DiCaprio in *Critters 3*

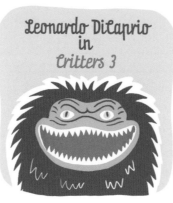

Jennifer Aniston in *Leprechaun*

Angelina Jolie in *Cyborg 2*

Sharon Stone in *Deadly Blessing*

Robert De Niro in *The Adventures of Rocky & Bullwinkle*

Demi Moore in *Parasite*

Nicole Kidman in *BMX Bandits*

George Clooney in *Return of the Killer Tomatoes*

Kevin Costner in just about all his movies after *The Bodyguard*.

Movie Sets We Can Visit in Real Life

The New York Municipal Library, the location of the first sighting of ectoplasm in *Ghostbusters*.

The Beverly Wilshire Hotel, Beverly Hills, where Richard Gere scored with Julia Roberts in *Pretty Woman*.

The childhood home of Luke Skywalker in *Star Wars* at Netfa in Tunisia, but you must hurry. It is disappearing under the sand.

Hugh Grant's book store in *Notting Hill* is now a London shoe store in the Notting Hill District, duh.

The Grail Temple or Temple of the Sun in *Indiana Jones and the Last Crusade* at Petra, in Jordan.

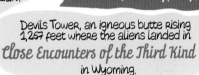

Devils Tower, an igneous butte rising 1,267 feet where the aliens landed in *Close Encounters of the Third Kind* in Wyoming.

The hill where Edward declares himself to Bella in *Twilight* just behind the Stone Cliff Inn in Oregon.

Kauai island in Hawaii where *Jurassic Park* was filmed.

The Hobbiton village in *The Lord of the Rings* at Matamata, New Zealand.

And as of 2016, we can explore a replica of the *Titanic* built by an Australian billionaire.

Why It's Worth the Trouble To Revisit *Wayne's World*

For the fascinating dialogue

If you set a fox free and she comes back, that's love! If you botch it and she takes off, it was never meant to be.

Benjamin is nobody's friend. If Benjamin were an ice cream flavor, he'd be pralines and dick.

For the vocabulary rich in neologisms

SCHWING!

Violent desire excited by the presence of the opposite sex.

PARTY-ON!

An exclamatory interjection expressing a mix of excitement and intense joy.

For the interesting classifications of feminine beauty

Baberaham Lincoln

Megababe

Bomb

Top Bomb

To watch Tia Carrere play the guitar

To see Alice Cooper in the role of Alice Cooper

For the best seduction scene of all time in *Wayne's World 2*, with Garth (Dana Carvey) and Honey Horneé (Kim Basinger)

The Actor Who Has Played the Most Number of Villains: Christopher Lee

(Incomplete list.)

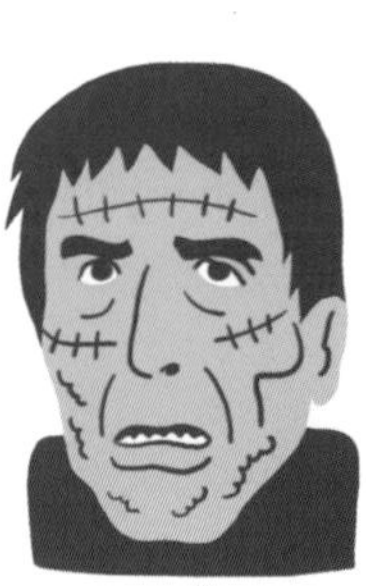

The Frankenstein monster
in *The Curse of Frankenstein.*

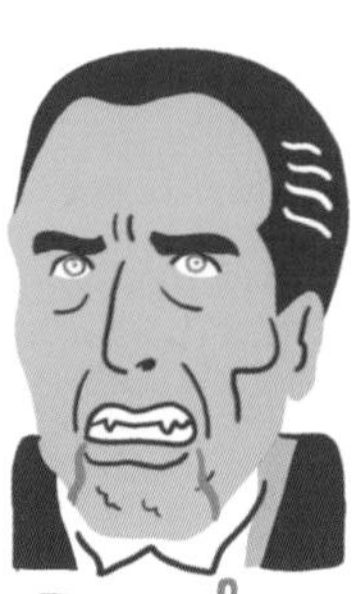

Dracula
in 11 movies.

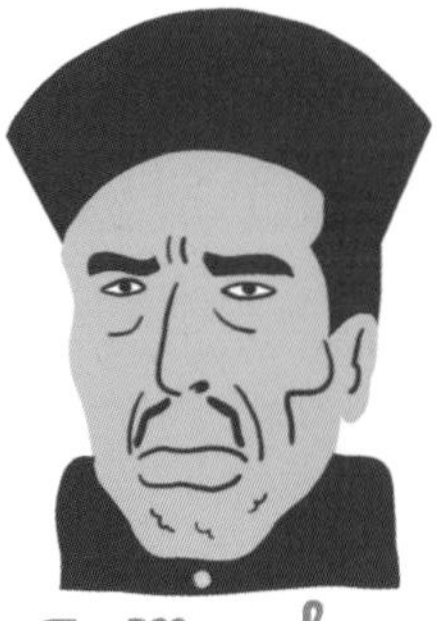

Fu Manchu
in 6 movies.

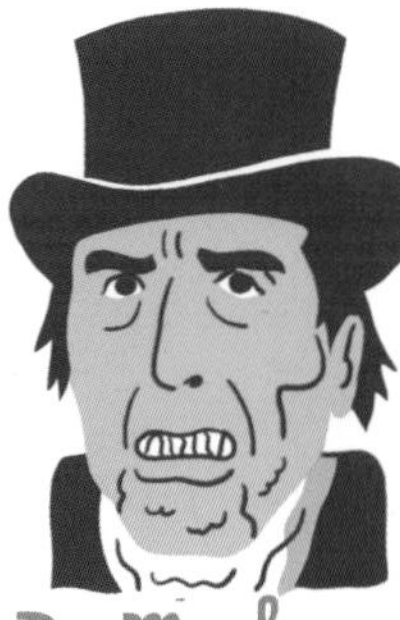

Dr. Marlowe
(Inspired by Dr. Jekyll)
in *I, Monster.*

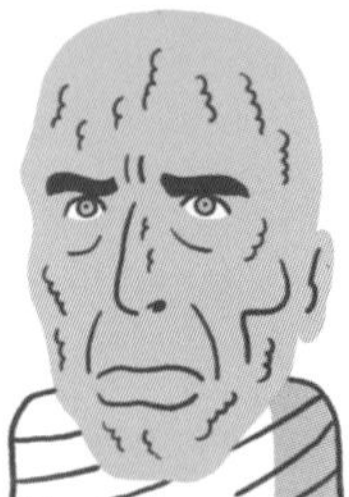

The Mummy
in *The Mummy.*

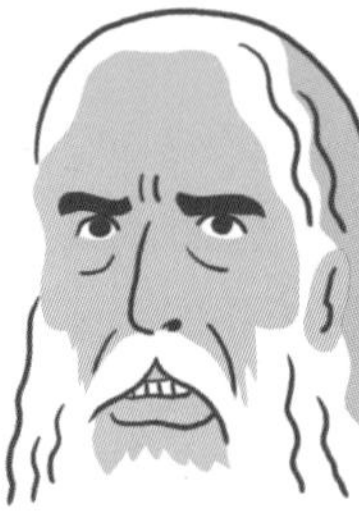

Rasputin
in *Rasputin the Mad Monk.*

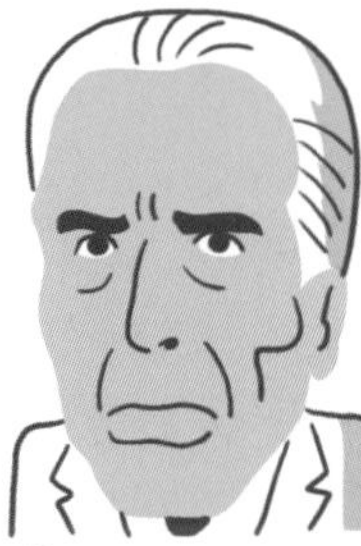

Scaramanga
in *James Bond: The Man with the Golden Gun.*

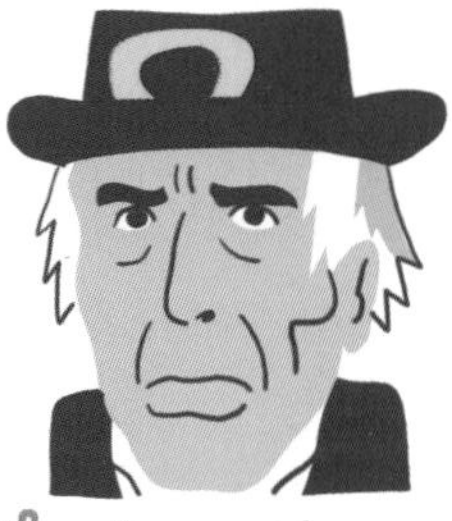

The Executioner
in *La Révolution française.*

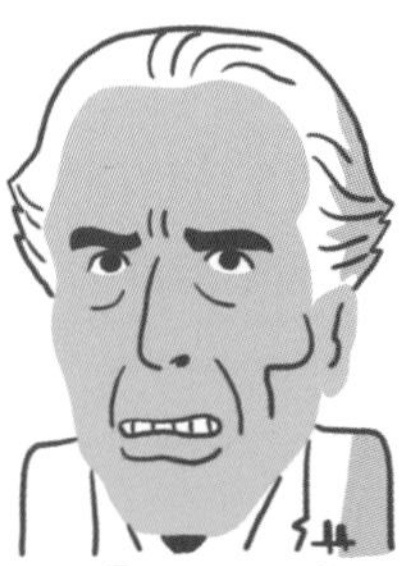

The Mad Scientist
in *Gremlins 2.*

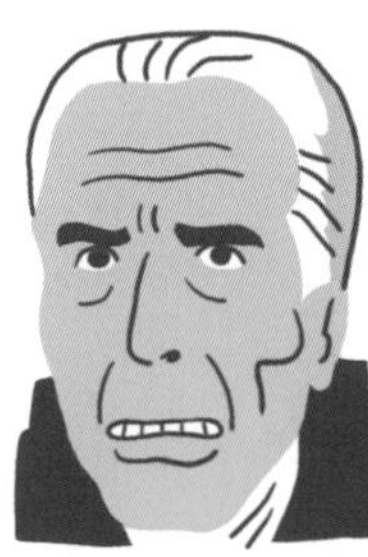

The Cruel Burgomaster
in *Sleepy Hollow.*

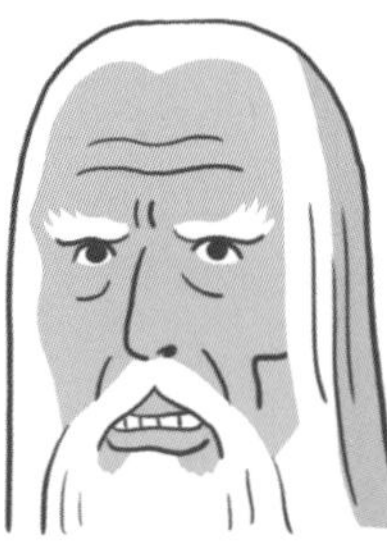

Saruman the White
in *The Lord of the Rings.*

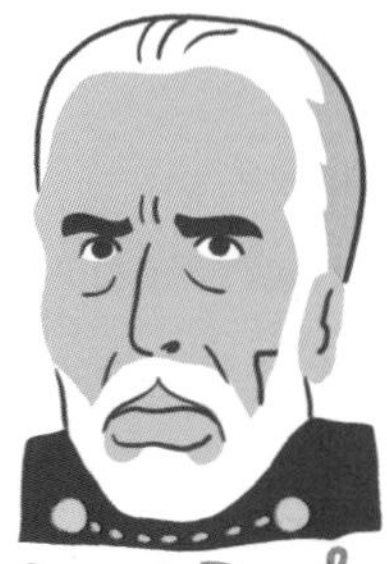

Count Dooku
in *Star Wars*, Episodes 2 and 3.

And he also recorded many symphonic heavy metal CDs, which is a really vile thing to do.

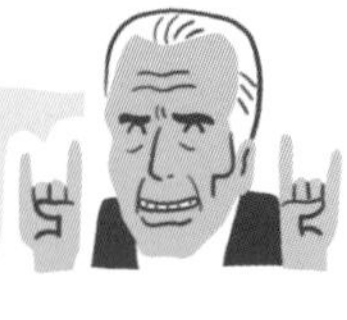

Proof That Obi-Wan Kenobi Is Completely Crazy

When he gives Anakin's lightsaber to Luke and tells him his father wanted him to have it... It's just not true – his father doesn't even know he exists.

When he tells Luke that his uncle didn't want Anakin to become a Jedi and fight in the war. No! Uncle Owen hadn't been born when Anakin left.

When he doesn't recall R2-D2 and C-3PO, both of whom he spent three movies with.

"I don't seem to remember ever owning a droid..."

When he said that Yoda was his Jedi Master. No! It was Qui-Gon Jinn.

When he says to Luke: "I haven't gone by the name Obi-Wan since oh, before you were born." No! In Episode 3, everyone called him Obi-Wan.

When he leaves Anakin on the ground beside a torrent of lava after cutting him to pieces. He didn't want to kill him so he leaves him to suffer a slow, agonizing death. That's niiice!

See ya!

When he says he "took it upon himself to train Anakin as a Jedi." Nope. Again it was Qui-Gon Jinn although Obi-Wan didn't agree to it.

As if I don't exist.

During the duel with Darth Vader, when he says to him, "If you strike me down, I shall become more powerful than you can imagine." Nonsense. He only becomes some kind of spook talking in Luke's head. Swell.

Bizarre Japanese Film Genres

Pinku eiga

Erotic films in which young, innocent women find themselves tied up in awkward positions.

Giri ninjo

Films featuring people torn between their moral values and their human feelings.

Chambara eiga

Films in which Samurai battle one other with swords.

Bake neko mono

Films with women who change into evil cats.

Kaijū eiga

Films with giant monsters that destroy cities.

Matatabi mono

Films whose hero is a brave yakuza with a mysterious past.

Tsuma mono

Films about brave housewives who succumb to sad outcomes.

Seishun eiga

Films featuring youth and their perennial problems, containing sex and violence.

The Worst Visions of the Future

Unbearable

Idiocracy
Human I.Q. has deteriorated dramatically and people spend their days seated on the toilet watching TV.

Gattaca
Your destiny is determined by your genome and everyone is dressed like a Calvin Klein fashion model.

Painful To Think About

Logan's Run
People live under geodesic domes and to avert overpopulation are terminated when they reach the age of 30.

Upsetting

Judge Dredd
Police officers make the law and perform on-the-spot executions for minor crimes, e.g., stealing a moped.

Soylent Green
People sleep in their cars and must eat their elders in the form of organic plankton.

Conceivable

The Postman
In a post-apocalyptic world, Kevin Costner is a mailman and saves the world with his horse.

Magical

Waterworld
In a post-apocalyptic submerged world, Kevin Costner is a mariner and saves the world with his trimaran.

Barb Wire
The USA is in the hands of neo-Nazis and Pamela Anderson is the only hope for humanity.

Film Projects That Never Saw the Light of Day and That's a Great Shame!

Night Skies
Directed by Steven Spielberg. Menacing aliens vs. White trash hicks.

Ilsa Meets Bruce Lee in the Devil's Triangle
The King of kung fu vs. a sick Nazi she-wolf.

Skaterella
Cinderella on roller skates in a musical comedy directed by Jacques Demy and produced by Francis Ford Coppola.

Dune
Directed by Alejandro Jodorowsky, with Mick Jagger and Salvador Dalí (who wanted to be paid $100,000 an hour).

Pippi Longstocking
By a young little-known Japanese animator back then (1971): Hayao Miyazaki.

The Little Prince
Directed by Orson Welles. A Disney production with Orson himself in the role of the aviator.

Napoleon
Directed by Stanley Kubrick, with Jack Nicholson in the role of the Emperor.

The Lord of the Rings
The Beatles version, with Paul McCartney as Frodo and John Lennon as Gollum.

Superman Lives
Directed by Tim Burton, with Nicolas Cage in the title role.

Actors Known for Only One Role

Mark Hamill in the role of Luke Skywalker.

Malcolm McDowell Alex in A Clockwork Orange.

Paul Hogan in the role of Crocodile Dundee.

Hayden Christensen in the role of Anakin Skywalker.

Christopher Reeve in the role of Superman.

Carrie Fisher in the role of Leia. (It's bad luck to play a Skywalker).

Leonard Nimoy in the role of Mr. Spock.

+ Actress Best Known for No Role in Particular:

Lindsay Lohan

Daniel Radcliffe in the role of Harry Potter. (Well, his career is not over, but we wish him a lot of luck.)

Actors Who Always Play the Same Role

Ben Stiller
A nice guy, but a bit of a wimp. You get the feeling that at any moment a piano will fall on his head.

Johnny Depp
The weird, mannered hero who always speaks as if on stage.

Morgan Freeman
The sage.

Kristen Stewart
The girl on Xanax who looks sad even when she's smiling.

Steven Seagal
The man of the hour who can break his opponent's neck while making an omelet.

Brad Pitt
The guy with the great hair.

Samuel L. Jackson
The mean-looking guy who could either be nice or evil or both.

Michael Cera
The clumsy teenager who is already 25 years old but seems predestined to remain a virgin forever.

Helena Bonham Carter
The unpredictable nutcase who might at any time slit her wrists with a laugh.

Woody Allen
Woody Allen.

Some Fun Easter Eggs

little, barely discernible inside jokes snuck into the movie by the director

In the opening scene of *Watchmen*, we can see Batman's parents (who have no reason to be there) escape from their gunman's attack.

In *Tron*, while Sark is staring intently at the control monitor, we see a little Pac-Man.

And also Mickey Mouse's head in the Solar Sailer simulation scene.

In *Toy Story*, the carpeting in Sid's house is the same as in the Overlook Hotel in *The Shining*.

And we see a license plate with the tag RN237, a reference to Room 237 where Jack Nicholson meets up with the ghost of the naked lady.

There are many subliminal images in *Fight Club* (including a concealed phallus towards the end), but have you noticed that in almost every scene, you see a Starbucks coffee cup?

In Mel Gibson's *Apocalypto*, in the scene where we see hundreds of massacred Indians on the ground, there is a fleeting image of an actor dressed as Waldo in *Where's Waldo?*

In *Raiders of the Lost Ark*, when Harrison Ford finds the Ark of the Covenant, we glimpse a hieroglyph of R2-D2 and C-3PO on the column to his right.

The Coolest Zombies

Zombie Sheep

Black Sheep
(2006)

Zombie Cheerleaders

Zombie
Cheerleading Camp
(2007)

Norwegian-Nazi Zombies

Dead Snow
(2009)

Backwoods-French Zombies

Villemolle 81
(2009)

Zombie Housewives

Flesh Eating Mothers
(1988)

Zombie Chickens

Poultrygeist: Night of
the Chicken Dead
(2006)

Zombie Schoolgirls

Stacy: Attack of the
Schoolgirl Zombies
(2001)

Zombie Bikers

Motocross Zombies
from Hell
(2007)

Zombie Farmers

Redneck Zombies
(1989)

Zombie Striptease Artists

Zombie Strippers
(2008)

Zombie Cops

Dead Heat
(1988)

Zombie Nudists

Nudist Colony
of the Dead
(1991)

More or Less Sexy Actors in a Skirt

Sean Connery
The Avengers
♡♡♡♡
The most hirsute.

Robin Williams
Mrs. Doubtfire
♡♡♡♡
The most motherly.

Christopher Lambert
Highlander
♥♡♡♡
The most everlasting.

Mel Gibson
Braveheart
♥♥♡♡
The most tartan.

Russell Crowe
Gladiator
♥♥♥♡
The most oiled.

Orlando Bloom
Troy
♥♥♡♡
The most mythological.

Tony Curtis
Spartacus
♥♡♡♡
The most ambivalent.

Dustin Hoffman
Tootsie
♥♥♥♥
The best.

Who Are These Serial Killers?

1 : Hannibal Lecter in *The Silence of the Lambs.* - 2 : Chucky in *Child's Play 2.*
3 : Norman Bates in *Psycho.* - 4 : Leatherface in *The Texas Chainsaw Massacre III.*
5 : Jigsaw in *Saw.* - 6 : Freddy Krueger in *A Nightmare on Elm Street.* - 7 : John Doe in *Seven.*
8 : Jason in *Friday the 13th.* - 9 : Monsieur Verdoux in *Monsieur Verdoux.*
10 : Michael Myers in *Halloween.* - 11 : Patrick Bateman in *American Psycho.*
12 : Sweeney Todd in *Sweeney Todd: The Demon Barber of Fleet Street.*

Movies Summed Up in One Sentence

The Lord of the Rings
A hobbit has to throw a ring into a volcano to save the world.

Cube
Some people unexpectedly find themselves in a cube and die.

Saw
John Kramer kills people over the course of 7 movies.

Zoolander
A fashion model who cannot do left turns on the runway saves the world.

Armageddon
Ben Affleck saves the world.

Daredevil
Ben Affleck saves the world in red tights.

Halloween
Michael Myers kills people in the course of 8 movies and 2 remakes.

Trainspotting
Drugs are bad.

Requiem for a Dream
Drugs are really, really bad.

Life of Pi
A teenager and a tiger are on a boat together.

Shaun of the Dead
Shaun is bored, and then suddenly there are zombies.

The Big Blue
Jacques Mayol wants to dive deeper than Enzo and dies as a result.

Bollywood Film Kit

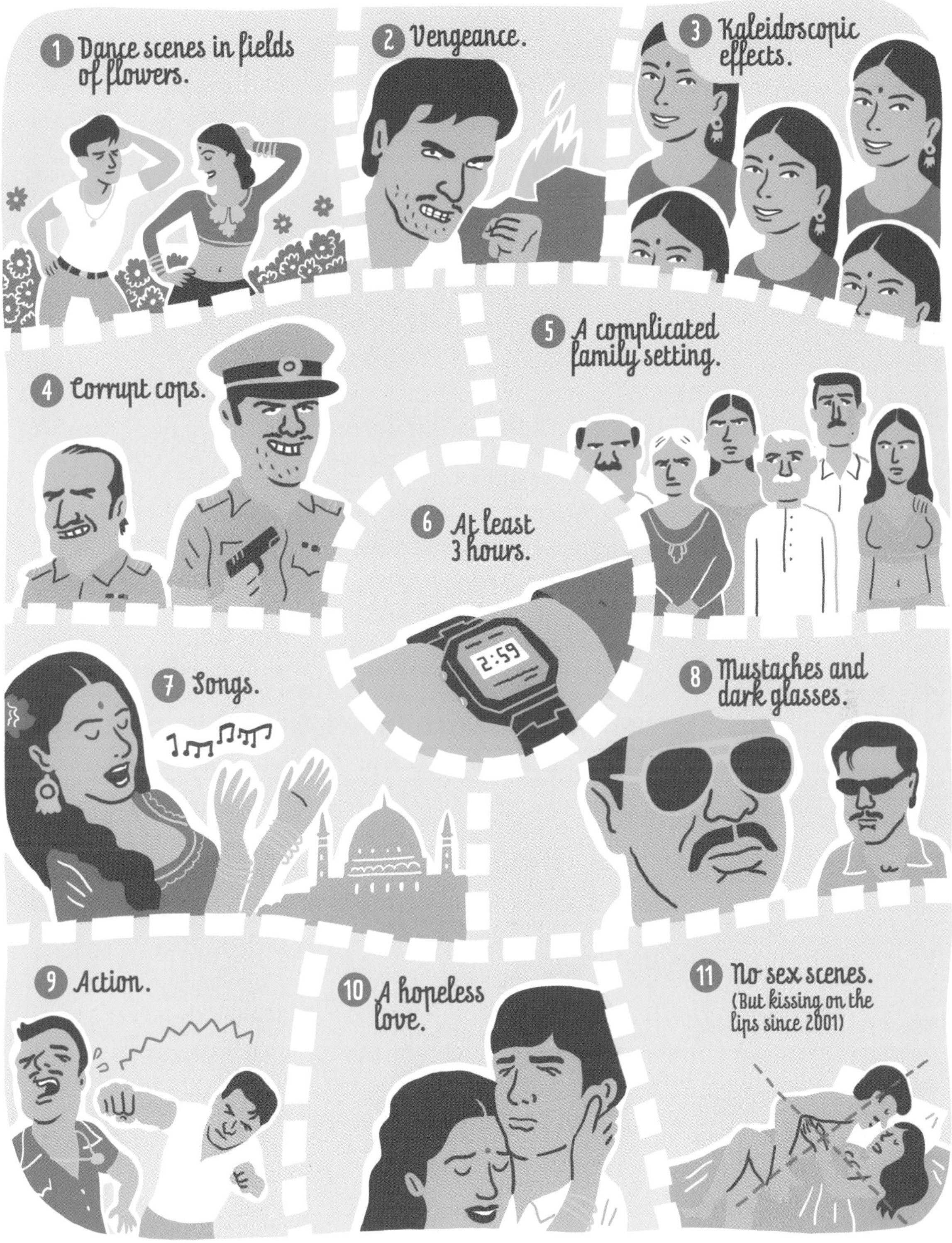
1 Dance scenes in fields of flowers.
2 Vengeance.
3 Kaleidoscopic effects.
4 Corrupt cops.
5 A complicated family setting.
6 At least 3 hours.
2:59
7 Songs.
8 Mustaches and dark glasses.
9 Action.
10 A hopeless love.
11 No sex scenes.
(But kissing on the lips since 2001)

Most Outrageously Erotic Image in a Movie That Just Isn't At All

Sigourney Weaver in *Alien*, when towards the end of the movie, she doffs her uniform and she's in bikini panties and a tight tee.

The Real Names of Those Animal Stars

Willy in Free Willy

Was called Keiko. After spending part of his life in marine parks, he was freed and lived out his life in a Norwegian fjord.

Lassie

Was a male called Pal. His offspring continued his role.

Beethoven

Was called Chris but died after the second film. His role was taken over by other St. Bernards.

Cheeta

Was called Jiggs in the first Tarzan movies. He also appeared with Laurel and Hardy and was buried in the Los Angeles Pet Memorial Park.

The Dolphin in The Big Blue

Was called Josephine and lived in Marineland in Antibes, to the age of 38, not bad for a dolphin.

Babe

Was played by 48 different pigs. (Because pigs grow very quickly.)

Flipper

Was a female called Mitzi. You can see her tombstone at the Florida Dolphin Research Center.

White Fang

Was called Jed and also played in The Thing.

Dexter the Capuchin Monkey in Night at the Museum

Was a female called Crystal. She was dubbed "Hollywood's Hottest Monkey" by USA Today and once during a shoot pooped on Robin Williams.

Old Movies with Monstrous Creatures Holding Fainting Damsels in their Arms

Ben Stiller vs Will Ferrell

Played a chair in an avant-garde theater piece, in his early years.	Played an elf in *Elf*.
Was fired from *Saturday Night Live* after only one season.	Was a backbone of *Saturday Night Live*.
Was elected "Best Male Model" three years in a row in *Zoolander*.	Was not re-elected in *The Campaign*.
Played alongside David Hasselhoff and William Shatner in *Dodgeball: A True Underdog Story*. He wasn't even injured!	Played alongside Mark Hamill and Carrie Fisher in *Jay and Silent Bob Strike Back*.
Played Attila the Hun in *Highway to Hell*.	Knows how to impersonate President George W. Bush.
Came face to face with Robert De Niro in *Meet the Parents*.	Was in one episode of *Man vs. Wild*, alongside Bear Grylls (the guy who eats live insect larvae).
Kissed Jennifer Aniston in *Along Came Polly*.	Kissed Sacha Baron Cohen in *Talladega Nights: The Ballad of Ricky Bobby*.
Was nominated for the most number of Golden Raspberry Awards in a single year (2004) for worst film.	Was nominated for the Golden Raspberry Award for the worst actor (*Land of the Lost*).
Has earned hundreds of millions in box-office returns.	Was crowned the least profitable Hollywood actor by Forbes.

The Coolest Cars Pt. 1

The Plymouth Fury in Christine

The Aston Martin DB5 in Goldfinger

The Pussy Wagon in Kill Bill

The Chevrolet Malibu in Drive

Herbie, the Volkswagen in the Herbie, the Love Bug series

The Ford Mustang GT in Bullitt

The amphibious Lotus Esprit S1 in The Spy Who Loved Me

The AMC Pacer "Garthmobile" in Wayne's World

The Batmobile, 1989 version

The Batmobile, 2005 version

Black Beauty, the Chrysler Imperial in The Green Hornet

The Coolest Cars Pt. 2

The Cadillac Ambulance in Ghostbusters

The Gran Torino in The Big Lebowski

The custom Ford Falcon in Mad Max

The Dodge Charger and the Toyota Supra in The Fast and the Furious

Austin Powers' Jaguar XK-E

Frankenstein's Alligator car in Death Race 2000

The Volkswagen Minibus in Little Miss Sunshine

The Ford Explorer in Jurassic Park

The DeLorean in Back to the Future

Things Possibly Overlooked Now That We Are at the End of this Book

Andy Serkis

is probably the most celebrated unknown actor. But he is a master of motion capture acting for such computer-generated characters as Gollum, King Kong, Captain Haddock and a chimp in *Planet of the Apes*.

My preciousss...

Michael Myers' Mask in *Halloween*

is in fact a Captain Kirk mask bought at a corner grocery store and painted white. The face of the killer in the series is therefore William Shatner's.

The Tragic End in *Titanic*

makes no sense whatsoever. Jack and Rose could have survived together on the raft, as we can prove here:

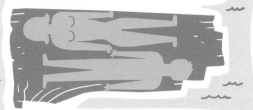

Course, if they had, they would've divorced in six months.

In *Galaxy Quest*

(1999)

there are some truly amazing things: old unemployed actors who save an extraterrestrial civilization and Sigourney Weaver as a blonde.

Who Played This Child?

1 Young Judy in *Jumanji*

2 Young Jim in *Empire of the Sun*

3 Young Grace in *The Horse Whisperer*

4 Young Norman in *A River Runs Through It*

1: Kirsten Dunst - 2: Christian Bale - 3: Scarlett Johansson - 4: Joseph Gordon-Levitt

The Wilhelm Scream

is a stock sound effect from the Warner Bros. Sound Effects Library that we hear in more than 200 films, such as *Star Wars*, *Indiana Jones*, *The Lord of the Rings*, *Batman* and even Tarantino's productions. Have a listen to it on YouTube, you'll know it.

Ah-aaah!

A movie made in 1984 that looks like it was made in the '40s with Bill Murray as the Captain of a lunar cruiser. It never made it to the theaters nor even to DVD. It exists and is called

Nothing Lasts Forever.

It's often said that Ed Wood's

Plan 9 from Outer Space

is the worst movie ever made, but if you believe that, you haven't seen *Day and Night* by Bernard-Henri Lévy.

Science fiction movies released the same year as the first *Star Wars* and were entirely lost to posterity:

 End of the World

 Cinderella 2000

 Starship Invasions

Planet of Dinosaurs

The War in Space

The self-lacing Nikes in *Back to the Future* are perhaps the coolest shoes in the history of movies, but there are also:

Beatrix Kiddo's Onitsuka Tiger Mexico 66 Slip-Ons in *Kill Bill*.

Data's Nike Sky Force Highs in *The Goonies*.

Axel Foley's Adidas Sambas in *Beverly Hills Cop*.

Forrest Gump's pair of Nike Classic Cortez.

The customized Nike Air Trainer IIIs in *Batman* (1989).

The custom Adidas Zissou Shoes in *The Life Aquatic with Steve Zissou*.

James Bond's
Dry Martini Recipe

- 3 parts vermouth
- 7 parts Vodka
- green spicy olives
- lemon peel
- ice cubes

Pour the vermouth and vodka into a shaker. Add ice and shake for 30 seconds while appearing casual. Serve with a lemon peel and decorate with a skewer of olives.

Recipe for the Wake-Up Juice Used To Resuscitate Doc Brown in *Back To The Future III*

- olive juice
- Tabasco sauce
- cayenne pepper
- red pepper
- minced onion
- mustard seeds

Place in mixer and stir well with a bit of water.
Bottoms up.
Resuscitate with care.

CINEGEEK

FUN TRIVIA TIDBITS CELEBRATING THE CINEMATIC WORLD